D0772213

TRAVEL & ADVENTURE

THE TRAVELS OF MARCO POLO

...UNDREDS OF YEARS AGO, EUROPE
...D A NUMBER OF BIG AND POWERFUL
...TIES. THEY WERE TRADING CENTERS
...H THEIR OWN ARMIES AND NAVIES...

Moby Dick
SEARCH FOR THE GREAT WHITE WHALE
HERMAN MELVILLE

GULLIVER'S TRAVELS

WORLD ALMANAC® LIBRARY

Please visit our Web site at: www.garethstevens.com
For a free color catalog describing World Almanac® Library's
list of high-quality books and multimedia programs,
call 1-800-848-2928 (USA) or 1-800-387-3178 (Canada).
World Almanac® Library's fax: (414) 332-3567.

Library of Congress Cataloging-in-Publication Data available upon request from publisher.
Fax (414) 336-0157 for the attention of the Publishing Records Department.

ISBN-13: 978-0-8368-7930-8 (lib. bdg.)
ISBN-13: 978-0-8368-7937-7 (softcover)

This North American edition first published in 2007 by
World Almanac® Library
A Member of the WRC Media Family of Companies
330 West Olive Street, Suite 100
Milwaukee, Wisconsin 53212 USA

"The Travels of Marco Polo" adapted by Seymour V. Reit, illustrated by Ernie Colón from *The Travels of Marco Polo* by Marco Polo and Rustichello of Pisa. Copyright © 1990 by Bank Street College of Education. Created in collaboration with *Boys' Life* magazine. First published in *Boys' Life* magazine, November 1990, by the Boy Scouts of America. Reprinted by permission of Bank Street College of Education and *Boys' Life* magazine.

"Moby Dick: Search for the Great White Whale" adapted by Seymour Reit, illustrated by Richard Rockwell, lettered by Shel Dorf from *Moby-Dick* by Herman Melville. Copyright © 1992 by Bank Street College of Education. Created in collaboration with *Boys' Life* magazine. First published in *Boys' Life* magazine, April 1992, by the Boy Scouts of America. Reprinted by permission of Bank Street College of Education and *Boys' Life* magazine.

"Gulliver's Travels" adapted by Seymour V. Reit, illustrated by Ernie Colón from *Gulliver's Travels* by Jonathan Swift. Copyright © 1990 by Bank Street College of Education. Created in collaboration with *Boys' Life* magazine. First published in *Boys' Life* magazine, February 1990, by the Boy Scouts of America. Reprinted by permission of Bank Street College of Education and *Boys' Life* magazine.

This U.S. edition copyright © 2007 by World Almanac® Library.

World Almanac® Library editorial direction: Mark Sachner
World Almanac® Library editors: Monica Rausch and Tea Benduhn
World Almanac® Library art direction: Tammy West
World Almanac® Library designer: Scott Krall
World Almanac® Library production: Jessica Yanke and Robert Kraus

Printed in Canada

1 2 3 4 5 6 7 8 9 10 10 09 08 07 06

THE TRAVELS OF MARCO POLO

NDREDS OF YEARS AGO, EUROPE
A NUMBER OF BIG AND POWERFUL
IES. THEY WERE TRADING CENTERS
H THEIR OWN ARMIES AND NAVIES.
1297, TWO OF THESE CITIES-- VENICE

PAGES 4-20

BANK STREET CLASSIC TALES

THE TRAVELS OF MARCO POLO

Adapted by Seymour V. Reit
Illustrated by Ernie Colón

HUNDREDS OF YEARS AGO, EUROPE HAD A NUMBER OF BIG AND POWERFUL CITIES. THEY WERE TRADING CENTERS WITH THEIR OWN ARMIES AND NAVIES. IN 1297, TWO OF THESE CITIES-- VENICE AND GENOA-- WENT TO WAR.

DURING THE FIGHTING, MANY VENETIANS WERE TAKEN PRISONER. ONE WAS A MAN NAMED MARCO POLO.

AFTER MANY DAYS TRAVELLING, WE CAME TO A TOWERING MOUNTAIN.

That's Mount Ararat, Marco.

Ararat? The Bible says this is where Noah's ark landed after the flood!

FROM THERE WE CONTINUED EAST UNDER A BLAZING SUN.

That isn't water. It's a substance called oil, gushing from a well.

Father, look! a fountain of black water!

People in this land burn it for fuel in their lamps. They also use it as a salve for skin ailments.

Hmm... I wonder if we'll ever use oil in our part of the world?

Back in his prison tower...

Good news, prisoners! A peace treaty has been signed. You can all go!

Now friends, you know of my travels— a journey that took twenty-four years, from start to finish.

But— but look at the jewels we brought back. This wool made from yak's fur. These stones that burn like wood.

FREE AT LAST, POLO TOOK THE BOOK THE SCRIBE HAD WRITTEN FOR HIM. MANY COPIES WERE MADE, BUT MOST PEOPLE DIDN'T BELIEVE WHAT THEY READ.

Your story is just a dream, Polo!

Signor Polo, do you wish to take back some of the incredible tales you've told?

IN 1324, AT THE AGE OF 70, MARCO POLO LAY ON HIS DEATH BED. A PRIEST LEANED OVER HIM.

No, Father, no. For I did not tell half of what I saw.

The End

19

MARCO POLO

MARCO POLO WAS AN ITALIAN MERCHANT WHOSE TALES OF HIS TRAVELS TO EASTERN ASIA WERE SOME OF THE FIRST ACCOUNTS MANY PEOPLE IN MEDIEVAL EUROPE HAD OF ASIA. POLO WAS BORN ON SEPTEMBER 15, 1254, IN VENICE, ITALY. HIS FATHER AND UNCLE LEFT VENICE TO TRAVEL EAST AND TRADE GOODS WITH THE MONGOLIAN EMPIRE (NOW MONGOLIA AND CHINA), HEADED BY KUBLAI KHAN. THEY RETURNED WHEN POLO WAS FIFTEEN YEARS OLD AND TOOK HIM BACK WITH THEM TO KHAN'S EMPIRE. ACCORDING TO POLO, THE THREE FOUND FAVOR WITH THE EMPEROR, AND POLO SERVED IN SEVERAL HIGH-RANKING POSITIONS IN THE EMPIRE. THEY RETURNED TO EUROPE WITH SEVERAL SHIPS AND CREW MEMBERS, ESCORTING A PRINCESS WHO WAS TO MARRY A MIDDLE EASTERN PRINCE. POLO, HIS FATHER, AND HIS UNCLE JOINED THE MILITARY WHEN VENICE FOUGHT A SHORT WAR WITH THE CITY-STATE OF GENOA. POLO WAS CAPTURED AS A WAR PRISONER IN 1298, AND, WHILE IN PRISON, HE DICTATED THE STORY OF HIS TRAVELS TO FELLOW PRISONER RUSTICHELLO OF PISA. RUSTICHELLO PUBLISHED THEM. AT THE TIME, MANY PEOPLE BELIEVED THE STORIES WERE EMBELLISHED OR FICTIONALIZED. TODAY, SOME EXPERTS BELIEVE POLO TRAVELED TO ONLY SOME OF THE PLACES HE MENTIONED. THE ACCOUNT OF HIS TRAVELS, HOWEVER, WAS PRINTED IN NUMEROUS LANGUAGES AND SPREAD THROUGHOUT EUROPE, AFFECTING HOW EUROPEANS THOUGHT OF ASIA AND ASIANS. CHRISTOPHER COLUMBUS HAD A GUIDE WITH HIM ON HIS OWN TRAVELS. AFTER POLO WAS RELEASED FROM PRISON, HE RETURNED TO VENICE, WHERE HE BECAME A WEALTHY MERCHANT. IN 1300, HE MARRIED DONATA BADOER. THEY HAD THREE CHILDREN TOGETHER. LATER, POLO WROTE A SECOND BOOK ABOUT HIS TRAVELS. THIS BOOK WAS QUICKLY TRANSLATED INTO LATIN AND OFTEN CREATED CONFLICTS WITH EDITIONS OF HIS FIRST BOOK. POLO DIED IN 1324 IN VENICE.

"Moby Dick"

SEARCH FOR THE GREAT WHITE WHALE

by HERMAN MELVILLE

MANY YEARS AGO MEN HUNTED WHALES WITH HAND-HELD SPEARS, RIDING IN SMALL WOODEN BOATS. THEIR VOYAGES WERE LONG, UNCOMFORTABLE, AND FILLED WITH CONSTANT DANGER. THIS IS THE STORY OF ONE SUCH VOYAGE-- A STRANGE TALE OF COURAGE, MADNESS, AND SUDDEN DEATH.......

Adapted by
SEYMOUR REIT

Illustrated by
RICHARD ROCKWELL

Lettered by
SHEL DORF

CALL ME ISHMAEL. SOME YEARS AGO, HAVING NO MONEY IN MY PURSE AND NOTHING TO KEEP ME ASHORE, I DECIDED TO SAIL ABOUT AND SEE THE WATERY PART OF THE WORLD.

SO I HEADED FOR A PORT CALLED NEW BEDFORD.

THERE IT IS! I'LL HAVE TO FIND SOME SHELTER FOR THE NIGHT

THIS LOOKS LIKE A PLACE WITH CHEAP LODGINGS.

SPOUTER INN
Peter Coffin
OWNER

AYE. WE'VE ROOM— BUT YE'LL HAVE TO SHARE A BED WITH ANOTHER SAILOR.

VERY WELL, BUT I DON'T MUCH FANCY THE IDEA.

MY BEDMATE WAS A HARPOONER, AND I TRIED TO STAY AWAKE UNTIL HE RETURNED.

IT'S NO USE, I'M MUCH... TOO... TIRED.

THEN, SEVERAL HOURS LATER...

WHO YOU? WHY IN MY BED? SPEAK OR I KILLEE!

LANDLORD! HO-HELP! SAVE ME!!

23

LATER I HELPED QUEEQUEG STORE SOME OF HIS BELONGINGS.

WH-WHAT'S THIS?

THAT-UM MY COFFIN.

YOUR C-COFFIN?

ME ALWAYS SAIL WITH COFFIN. QUEEQUEG KILLEE WHALE, BUT MEBBE WHALE KILLEE QUEEQUEG!

FOR SEVERAL DAYS AFTER LEAVING NANTUCKET, NOTHING WAS SEEN OF CAPTAIN AHAB.

WHERE'S OUR LEADER, MR. STARBUCK?

LURKING IN HIS CABIN, ISHMAEL. HE'S AN ODD ONE.

THEN ONE MORNING, AS I CAME UP FROM BELOW...

IT'S HIM ON THE QUARTER-DECK, CAPTAIN AHAB!

HE STOOD AND STARED, WITH A LOOK ON HIS SCARRED FACE AS IF A THOUSAND DEMONS WERE TORMENTING HIM.

THEN I SAW HIS PEG LEG--MADE OF IVORY, CARVED FROM A WHALE'S JAWBONE!

MR. STARBUCK, CALL ALL THE HANDS AFT.

AYE, AYE, CAP'N!

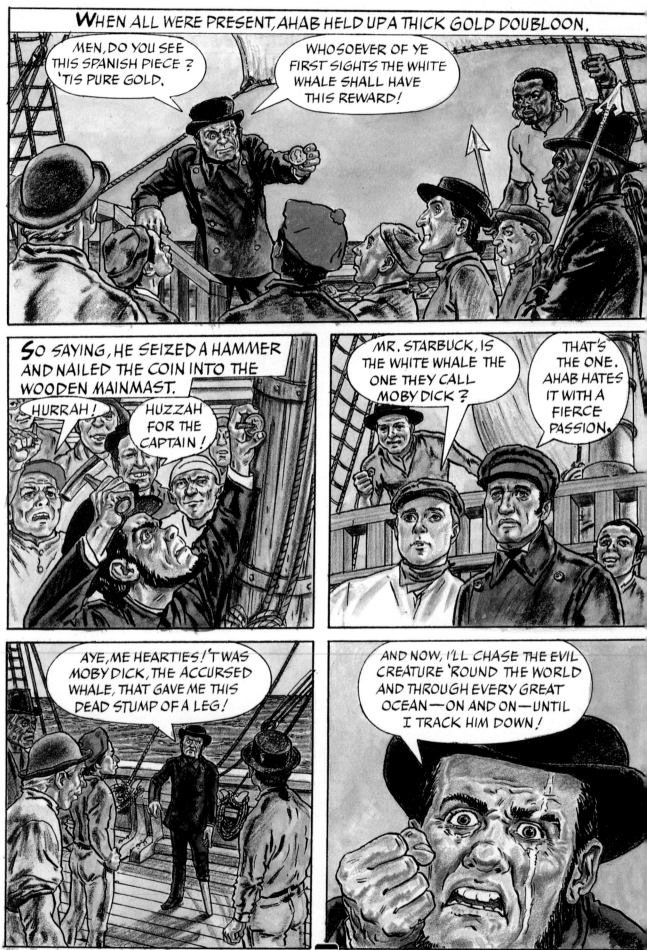

SAILING INTO THE PACIFIC, WE CAME UPON ANOTHER WHALING SHIP, THE "RACHEL", AND AHAB HAILED HER.

AHOY! HAVE YE SEEN ANY SIGN OF AN EVIL WHITE WHALE WITH A CROOKED JAW?

NO, BUT A SCHOOL OF SPERM WHALES IS LYING DUE EAST!

SOON THERE WAS A CRY FROM OUR LOOKOUT ON THE MASTHEAD.

WHALES OFF! WHALES OFF! A WHOLE PASSEL OF 'EM, CAPTAIN!

THIS TIME, STUBB'S BOAT WAS IN THE LEAD, WITH TASHTEGO AS HIS HARPOONER.

Ault Colorado

TAKING TWO OF TASHTEGO'S HARPOONS, THE WHALE RUSHED THROUGH THE SEA, CARRYING THE MEN ON A "NANTUCKET SLEIGH RIDE!"

AT LAST THE CREATURE GREW TIRED. THE WHALE BOAT CLOSED IN AND STUBB THRUST HIS LANCE TO THE WHALE'S HEART.

STRIPS OF BLUBBER WERE THEN CUT FROM THE DEAD BEAST AND BOILED DOWN IN IRON VATS CALLED "TRY POTS."

FOR MANY DAYS WE HARPOONED THESE WHALES AND SOON THE SHIP'S HOLD WAS JAMMED WITH HUGE BARRELS OF WHALE OIL.

WE HAVE A FULL CARGO, CAP'N. SHALL I GIVE ORDERS TO SAIL FOR HOME?

NEVER! WE'RE NOT TURNING BACK UNTIL THE WHITE WHALE IS MINE!

AT THAT MOMENT STARBUCK SAW THE TRUTH.

THE MAN'S MAD. HE MAY LEAD US ALL TO OUR DOOM.

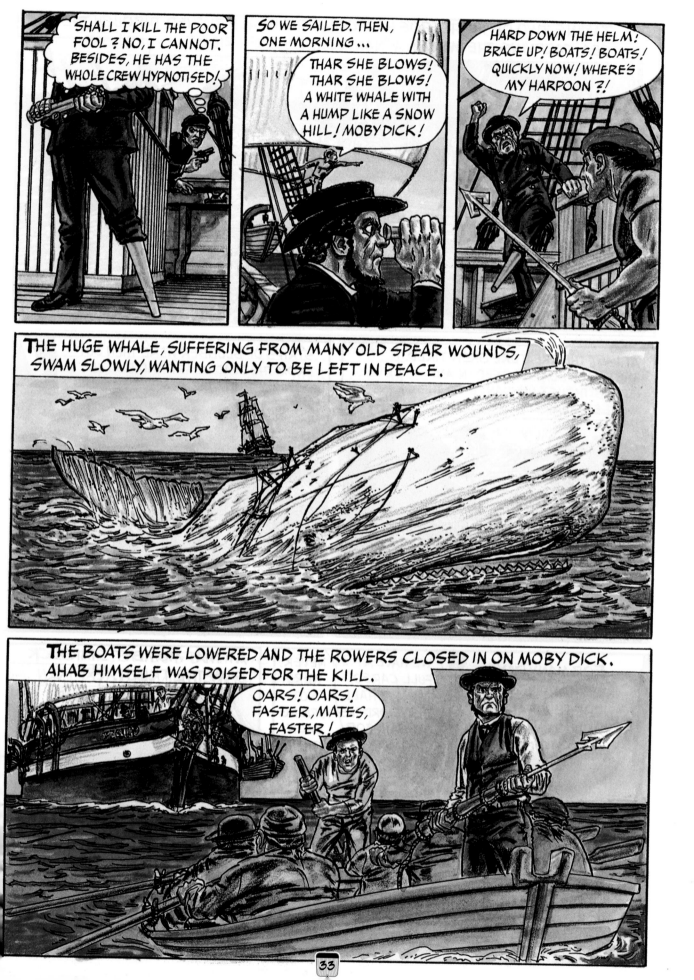

SUDDENLY THE OCEAN HEAVED. WITH A MIGHTY RUSH OF WAVE AND FOAM, THE WHITE WHALE LUNGED FROM THE SEA! MADDENED BY PAIN, HE SMASHED HIS POWERFUL HEAD INTO THE HULL OF OUR SHIP. MOBY DICK HIT THE SHIP AGAIN AND AGAIN UNTIL IT BEGAN TO SPLINTER LIKE MATCHWOOD.

HERMAN MELVILLE

ALTHOUGH HERMAN MELVILLE WAS NOT A WELL-KNOWN AUTHOR DURING HIS LIFETIME, HIS NOVEL **MOBY-DICK** SINCE HAS BECOME A CLASSIC AMERICAN MASTERPIECE. MELVILLE WAS BORN ON AUGUST 1, 1819, IN NEW YORK CITY. HE SURVIVED AN ILLNESS IN HIS CHILDHOOD THAT LEFT HIM WITH POOR EYESIGHT. AT AGE TWELVE, AFTER HIS FATHER DIED AND LEFT THE FAMILY IN POVERTY, MELVILLE WENT TO WORK. ALTHOUGH HE WAS NOT IN SCHOOL, HE CONTINUED TO STUDY ON HIS OWN AND READ HISTORY AND SCIENCE BOOKS IN HIS FREE TIME. HE WORKED AS A CLERK, A FARMHAND, AND, LATER, A TEACHER. MELVILLE, HOWEVER, LONGED TO TRAVEL, AND IN 1839, HE JOINED A WHALING SHIP AS A CABIN BOY. HE THEN SPENT SEVERAL YEARS TRAVELING THE OCEANS. HE RETURNED TO NEW YORK AND BEGAN TO WRITE STORIES BASED ON HIS TRAVELS. HIS FIRST NOVEL, **TYPEE**, WAS PUBLISHED IN 1846 AND WAS A HUGE SUCCESS. HE FOLLOWED IT WITH **OMOO** IN 1847. HIS NEXT BOOK, HOWEVER, WAS NOT AS POPULAR. HE WORKED FOR SEVERAL YEARS WRITING **MOBY-DICK** (1851), WEAVING REFERENCES TO BIBLE STORIES INTO THE TALE. **MOBY-DICK**, HOWEVER, WAS NOT GREETED WELL BY THE PUBLIC. AFTER SEVERAL MORE NOVELS, MELVILLE GREW DISCOURAGED AND, FOR A TIME, WROTE ONLY POETRY. HE MARRIED ELIZABETH SHAW AND HAD FOUR CHILDREN. BY 1857, HE WAS FORCED TO TAKE A JOB AS A CUSTOMS INSPECTOR TO SUPPORT HIS FAMILY. HE DIED IN 1891, AS A RELATIVELY UNKNOWN AUTHOR. IN THE 1920S, MANY PEOPLE BEGAN TO STUDY HIS WORK, AND HE SOON BECAME RECOGNIZED AS AN IMPORTANT AMERICAN AUTHOR.

THE TRAVELS OF MARCO POLO

HUNDREDS OF YEARS AGO, EUROPE
[HA]D A NUMBER OF BIG AND POWERFUL
[CIT]IES. THEY WERE TRADING CENTERS
[WIT]H THEIR OWN ARMIES AND NAVIES.
[IN 1]297, TWO OF THESE CITIES— VENICE

Moby Dick
SEARCH FOR THE GREAT WHITE WHALE

GULLIVER'S TRAVELS

GULLIVER'S TRAVELS

by Jonathan Swift

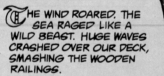

THE WIND ROARED. THE SEA RAGED LIKE A WILD BEAST. HUGE WAVES CRASHED OVER OUR DECK, SMASHING THE WOODEN RAILINGS.

IT WAS THE WORST STORM THAT I, LEMUEL GULLIVER, HAD EVER SEEN... AND IT HAD SWEPT ME INTO A STRANGE, MAD ADVENTURE... ONE I CAN STILL HARDLY BELIEVE.

LET ME TELL YOU HOW IT ALL CAME ABOUT...

BANK STREET CLASSIC TALES
adapted by:
Seymour V. Reit
illustrated by:
Ernie Colón

40

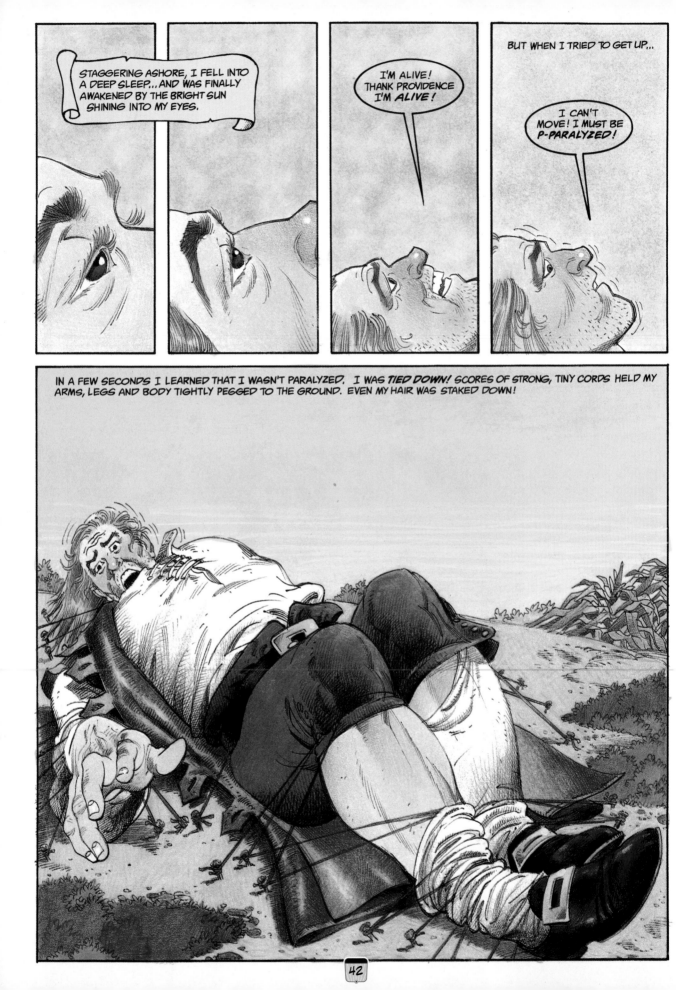

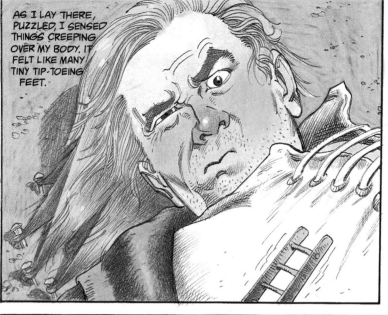

AS I LAY THERE, PUZZLED, I SENSED THINGS CREEPING OVER MY BODY. IT FELT LIKE MANY TINY TIP-TOEING FEET.

I FORCED MY HEAD UP TO SEE... AND WHAT I SAW WAS A TINY HUMAN CREATURE, SIX INCHES HIGH!

MEKINA DEGUL!

BEHIND HIM I COULD MAKE OUT OTHER TINY HUMANS! I WAS SO ASTONISHED, I GAVE A GREAT ROAR...

ARRHH!

...WHICH TO THEM SOUNDED LIKE A VAST CLAP OF THUNDER. FRIGHTENED, THEY RAN OFF HELTER-SKELTER!

ONE FAT FELLOW IN A UNIFORM LOST HIS BALANCE AND LANDED IN THE MUD.

HE WAS EMBARRASSED BY HIS FALL AND HELD ME TO BLAME. THIS WAS ADMIRAL BOLGOLAM, WHO WOULD BECOME MY MORTAL ENEMY.

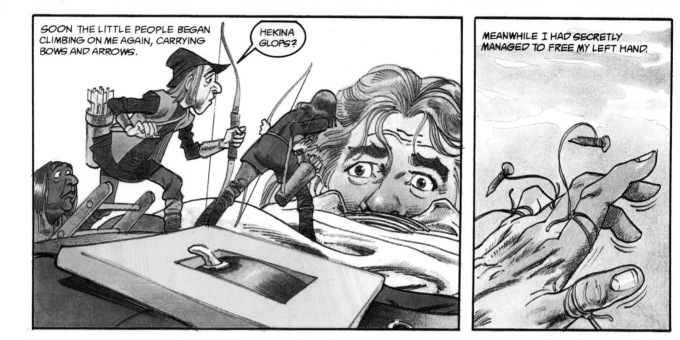

SOON THE LITTLE PEOPLE BEGAN CLIMBING ON ME AGAIN, CARRYING BOWS AND ARROWS.

HEKINA GLOPS?

MEANWHILE I HAD SECRETLY MANAGED TO FREE MY LEFT HAND.

I MADE A QUICK SWIPE AT ONE OF THE ARCHERS. SPRY AS A GRASSHOPPER, HE LEAPED BACK TO SAFETY.

KLOOB!

IMMEDIATELY HIS FELLOW ARCHERS BEGAN TO FIRE ARROWS AT MY FACE! BUT I MANAGED TO PROTECT MY EYES WITH MY FREE HAND.

TOLGO PHONAC!

THE ARROWS STUNG BADLY, AND I WAS WORRIED ABOUT MY EYES. SO I MADE SIGNS OF SURRENDER.

STOP! NO MORE! I GIVE UP!

THE TINY ONES UNDERSTOOD AND STOPPED THEIR ATTACK. SOME WOMEN PULLED OUT THE ARROWS AND RUBBED ON A SOOTHING OINTMENT.

44

THEN, BEFORE MY STARTLED GAZE, CAME A LONG LINE OF CHEFS. I LEARNED THAT THEY'D BEEN COOKING FOOD FROM THE MOMENT I WAS DISCOVERED. EACH BASKET WAS FILLED WITH MINIATURE LEGS OF MUTTON AND ROAST CHICKENS.

BEHIND THEM CAME BAKERS PUSHING CARTS PILED WITH LOAVES OF BREAD. EACH LOAF WAS THE SIZE OF A MUSKET BALL.

FINALLY ANOTHER GROUP BROUGHT BARRELS OF LIQUID. THE BARRELS WERE ABOUT THE SIZE OF THIMBLES.

WHILE THEY STARED IN AMAZEMENT, I GULPED DOWN THE TASTY FOOD AND DRANK A DOZEN BARRELS OF THEIR DELICIOUS FRUIT CIDER.

WATCH OUT BELOW!

THUD!

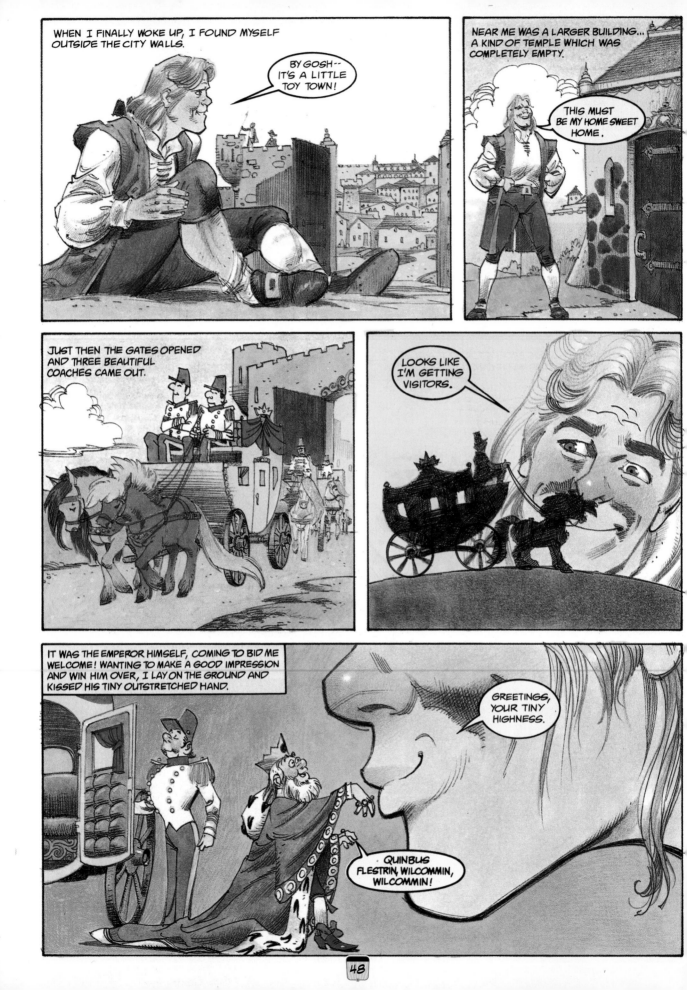

I TOOK OUT BIG BOULDERS WHERE FARMERS WERE CLEARING THE LAND.

FROM THEN ON I WAS THEIR FRIEND AND ALLY. THE WEE PEOPLE FED ME WELL AND I, IN TURN, AIDED THEM IN MANY WAYS.

I ALSO PULLED OUT MANY TALL TREES, HELPING THE ENGINEERS BUILD A ROAD.

THE EMPEROR SENT A FAMOUS PROFESSOR TO TEACH ME THEIR LANGUAGE, AND I LEARNED IT QUICKLY.

HOW DO YOU DO?--BLUB GUMDRUM--

HOW DO YOU DO?--BLUB GUMDRUM--

I LEARNED THAT THIS ISLAND WAS CALLED "LILLIPUT". AND THEIR NAME FOR ME WAS "QUINBUS FLESTRIN," WHICH MEANS *MAN MOUNTAIN!*

ONE NIGHT THE ROYAL PALACE CAUGHT ON FIRE AND THERE WAS GREAT ALARM!

HURRYING OVER AS BEST I COULD, I PULLED OFF MY LEATHER VEST...

STAND BACK!

...AND USED IT TO SMOTHER THE FIRE QUICKLY.

49

CARRYING MY HOOKS, I WADED INTO THE WATER TOWARD THE BLEFUSCU NAVY.

WHEN THE SAILORS SAW ME COMING, THEY HOWLED WITH FEAR, LEAPED OVERBOARD, AND SWAM ASHORE.

TAKING MY TIME, I ATTACHED A HOOK TO THE PROW OF EACH SHIP.

THEN, HOLDING ALL THE ROPES TOGETHER IN ONE HAND, I TURNED BACK TO LILLIPUT, PULLING THE ENTIRE BLEFUSCU NAVY BEHIND ME!

SING HO -- SING HO -- SING HO FOR THE LIFE OF A SAILOR!

WITH THIS LITTLE VICTORY I BECAME A BIGGER HERO THAN EVER, AND THE EMPEROR STAGED A GRAND PARADE IN MY HONOR...

QUINBUS FLESTRIN

QUINBUS FLESTRIN

OF COURSE ADMIRAL BOLGOLAM WAS GREEN WITH ENVY. BY CAPTURING THE ENEMY FLEET, I HAD PUT HIM TO SHAME.

INSTEAD OF PARADING, HE MET WITH HIS EVIL COMRADES. LITTLE DID I KNOW THAT THEY WERE PLOTTING MY DOWNFALL.

Lilliput Inn

THAT NIGHT, I HAD A SECRET VISIT FROM LORD HURGO...

PSST! PSST! QUINBUS!

...WHO WARNED ME THAT MY LIFE WAS IN DANGER!

FLESTRIN KAPUT!

52

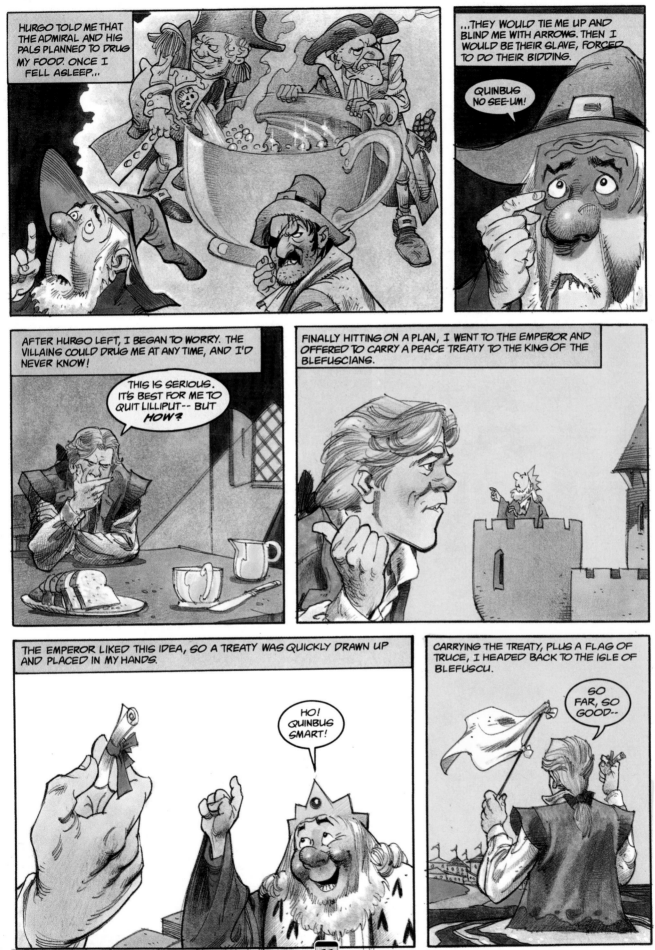

HURGO TOLD ME THAT THE ADMIRAL AND HIS PALS PLANNED TO DRUG MY FOOD. ONCE I FELL ASLEEP...

...THEY WOULD TIE ME UP AND BLIND ME WITH ARROWS. THEN I WOULD BE THEIR SLAVE, FORCED TO DO THEIR BIDDING.

QUINBUS NO SEE-UM!

AFTER HURGO LEFT, I BEGAN TO WORRY. THE VILLAINS COULD DRUG ME AT ANY TIME, AND I'D NEVER KNOW!

THIS IS SERIOUS. IT'S BEST FOR ME TO QUIT LILLIPUT-- BUT *HOW*?

FINALLY HITTING ON A PLAN, I WENT TO THE EMPEROR AND OFFERED TO CARRY A PEACE TREATY TO THE KING OF THE BLEFUSCIANS.

THE EMPEROR LIKED THIS IDEA, SO A TREATY WAS QUICKLY DRAWN UP AND PLACED IN MY HANDS.

HO! QUINBUS SMART!

CARRYING THE TREATY, PLUS A FLAG OF TRUCE, I HEADED BACK TO THE ISLE OF BLEFUSCU.

SO FAR, SO GOOD--

THE SHIP CAME CLOSER, HOVE TO, AND I HAPPILY CLIMBED ABOARD.

HER MASTER, CAPTAIN BIDDEL, WAS MOST KIND AND HELPFUL.

WE'RE BOUND FOR ENGLAND, DOCTOR. WE'LL GIVE YOU SAFE PASSAGE.

I'M IN YOUR DEBT. THANK YOU.

LATER IN HIS CABIN, I TOLD BIDDEL OF MY ADVENTURES...THE SHIPWRECK, COMING TO LILLIPUT, THE NAVAL VICTORY, THE PLOT, EVERYTHING.

HE STARED AT ME SILENTLY FOR A MOMENT. THEN...

HEE HEE! HOO! YOU SPIN A *FINE YARN*, DOCTOR! TINY PEOPLE! HA HA!

BUT-- BUT--

HAW HAW! A GRAND *WHOPPER!* YOU MADE IT SOUND ALMOST *REAL!* HEE HEE HEE!

ᔕERE ENDS MY STORY. TRUE TO HIS PROMISE, THE CAPTAIN CARRIED ME SAFELY HOME. BUT I COULD NEVER CONVINCE HIM THAT MY WILD ADVENTURE WAS A TRUE ONE.

BACK IN LONDON, IT WAS THE SAME. NOT A SOUL BELIEVED MY STRANGE TALE! AND LATELY I'VE BEGUN TO WONDER. *DID* IT ALL HAPPEN TO ME? OR WAS IT MERELY THE WORKING OF A CASTAWAY'S FEVERED MIND?

I DON'T KNOW... I DON'T KNOW. *IS* THERE AN INCREDIBLE RACE OF TINY HUMANS OUT THERE ... SOMEWHERE?

WHAT DO *YOU* THINK?

SIGNED THIS DAY,

Lemuel Gulliver

THE END

JONATHAN SWIFT

JONATHAN SWIFT WAS AN ANGLO-IRISH AUTHOR AND CLERGYMAN WHO WAS KNOWN FOR HIS USE OF SATIRE. SWIFT WAS BORN ON NOVEMBER 30, 1667, IN DUBLIN, IRELAND. HIS FATHER DIED JUST MONTHS BEFORE HE WAS BORN, AND HIS MOTHER LEFT HIM IN THE CARE OF HIS FATHER'S WEALTHY BROTHER. SWIFT ATTENDED KILKENNY GRAMMAR SCHOOL AND, LATER, TRINITY COLLEGE, GRADUATING IN 1686. HE THEN WENT TO ENGLAND, WHERE HE WORKED AS A SECRETARY FOR SIR WILLIAM TEMPLE, AN ENGLISH DIPLOMAT AND NOBLEMAN. WHILE HE WORKED FOR TEMPLE, SWIFT EARNED A MASTER'S DEGREE AT OXFORD UNIVERSITY. HE WAS ALSO ORDAINED A MINISTER IN THE ANGLICAN CHURCH OF IRELAND IN 1695.

SWIFT HAD HOPED THAT HIS WORK FOR TEMPLE WOULD LEAD TO A MORE POWERFUL POLITICAL POSITION, BUT TEMPLE DIED BEFORE SWIFT'S HOPES WERE REALIZED. SWIFT RETURNED TO IRELAND TO SERVE AS THE VICAR, OR MINISTER, OF LARACOR. FOR THE NEXT SEVERAL YEARS, HE GAINED SOME FAME THROUGH PUBLISHING SEVERAL SATIRICAL ESSAYS ON POLITICAL AND RELIGIOUS ISSUES AND, IN 1704, A RELIGIOUS SATIRE CALLED **A TALE OF A TUB**. HE TRAVELED BACK AND FORTH BETWEEN ENGLAND AND IRELAND AND OFTEN WORKED AS A POLITICAL ACTIVIST. AFTER THE DEATH OF QUEEN ANNE IN 1714, THE POLITICAL PARTY WITH WHOM SWIFT HAD ALIGNED HIMSELF FELL OUT OF POWER. HE RETURNED TO IRELAND DISAPPOINTED. SWIFT BEGAN TO WRITE **GULLIVER'S TRAVELS** IN 1720 AND PUBLISHED IT IN 1726. THE BOOK WAS AN INSTANT SUCCESS. HIS MATTER-OF-FACT WAY OF PRESENTING THE EXPERIENCES OF GULLIVER WITH GIANTS AND LITTLE PEOPLE LED MANY READERS TO BELIEVE THEY WERE REAL. HIS OTHER WORKS INCLUDED **THE DRAPIER'S LETTERS** (1724) AND **A MODEST PROPOSAL** (1729). SWIFT WAS RUMORED TO HAVE MARRIED, IN 1716, HIS FORMER STUDENT ESTHER "STELLA" JOHNSON, BUT HE DID NOT HAVE ANY CHILDREN. THROUGHOUT HIS LIFE, SWIFT SUFFERED FROM SPELLS OF DIZZINESS AND NAUSEA AND FROM HEARING LOSS. HE DIED IN 1745, AFTER SEVERAL YEARS OF ILLNESS.